The Effective Leader

Leading the way to success

William A. Newman
Training Consultant

"Leadership and learning are indispensable to each other."

Prologue

As leaders, we must act in concert with our beliefs and values. Being effective leaders is one of the greatest challenges that we face each day. It holds true for leaders of all walks of life and equally true for organizations of any size and industry type.

Most organizations promote good management through their stated mission, vision and values. These displays of good intentions are excellent reminders of what we stand for. But the real worth of our values comes from what is practiced rather than what we talk about. Its how we actually *behave* that ultimately defines our success as leaders and determines how we will be judged.

The purpose of this guide is to help you determine what makes an effective leader and assist you in using this to further develop yourselves. We will introduce leadership skills and characteristics you can measure yourself against and offer practical strategies to add to your existing value-driven leadership practices. As you begin to apply the ideas and techniques in this reference book, remember that this is a journey and not a destination. The fact that you may never fully arrive is not important. What is important is for you to continue moving in the right direction.

If you believe you can make a difference, then you probably will.

A Leader's Profile

Leaders come in all shapes, sizes and personalities. We are our own best role model when it comes to being an effective leader. The best benchmark we can use on our journey to becoming an effective leader is our own best behavior.

Simply put, is that if we strip away all but the essentials, being an effective leader is about knowing ourselves. Knowing our strengths, our shortcomings, what gives us pleasure and what annoys us the most. Knowing why we go to work, why we react as we do under pressure, what scares us and what make us proud. The truly effective leaders we know all have one thing in common, if nothing else: *They know themselves very well.*

Self-knowledge is fundamental to being an effective leader for one simple reason: *trust is built on honesty.* If we are to be trusted about matters of strategy, staffing, marketing, mentoring, etc...we must first be able to understand what our natural tendencies are, and why in some situations, those tendencies work for us, and why in other situations, they work against us. We must be comfortable in our own skin and we must also be able to share our understanding of ourselves with others, so that their expectations will be in line with our delivery. Above all else, an effective leader means *not faking it.*

Let's dig a little deeper into what we mean by self-knowledge. We mean having the ability to say that we are a people person, or not – that we are tech savvy, or not – that we are a perfectionist or lazy – patient or impatient. That we avoid conflict whenever possible, or that we enjoy a good argument. Once we understand our strengths and weaknesses in some depth, we can then step back and consider how our personal makeup works when it is applied in the many roles we take on as a leader.

Does our preference to deal with data rather than people work for us or against us when we are analyzing the market? How about when we are facilitating a discussion? Working with a client? Monitoring our company performance? Mentoring an employee?

Once we understand how our own personal makeup works, for, or against us in our various leadership roles, we can then begin to figure out how to use our strengths and compensate for our weaknesses while maintaining our integrity.

Too often, we see people who would otherwise be trustworthy and who would otherwise be perceived as an effective leader – run into trouble in trying to overcompensate for a weakness. They put on a 'game face' that is very easy to see through. An awkward personal comment from the manager who is, by nature not a people person but who is trying to seem so during a pep talk or a forced tone of gratitude in a speech made by someone who is not really grateful or a false sense of enthusiasm from someone who is not demonstrative. None of this works.

But just because we might not be particularly good at one or another style of leadership does not mean we can't be trusted. Just because we have to try harder in certain areas doesn't mean we are not able to be an effective leader. Do we by nature, avoid conflict? Do we do whatever we can to avoid delivering hard messages? That doesn't mean that we won't deliver those messages when we have to. It means that we have to work harder at being able to do it with some level of comfort. Or it means that we have to find an appropriate delivery mechanism to support or supplement our efforts.

Let people see that some things don't come naturally for us. Let people see that we're trying to improve in certain areas. Assume that we are a quiet person by nature. As long as we can even say something like: "It's hard for me to be boisterous. I can't froth at the mouth. But I can tell you how pleased or angry something makes me. I can express it. I can demonstrate it in other ways", that's fine. We'll be doing something called "name it and claim it," which is a *big trust builder*. What's critical is that we're not faking a level of comfort that we don't actually feel.

What happens if we do fake it? Eventually we'll be faking it more and more and our fake self will be the person that people expect to see. If that's the case, if we're in a role that we really feel calls for the portrayal of a person we're not – doesn't that tell us something about our 'fit' at our place of employment? Isn't it telling us something about our life? Isn't that a signal we should pay attention to? There are numerous ways of developing that self-knowledge, or coming to terms with who we are.

One good way to gain self-knowledge is to spend some time thinking about what motivates us. Studies have shown that most people's motivation stems from some combination of the following four sources:

➢ Duty
➢ Meaning
➢ Accomplishment
➢ Happiness

Why do we go to work each day? Is it mostly to put food on the table and pay our mortgage? Do we work because we feel that what we do genuinely makes a positive difference in the world? Do we want to see how far up the ladder we can climb? Do we work because we love what we do?

The key is being honest with our answers. There is no right or wrong response. There is no right or wrong mix. If duty is our lead motivator and it is rooted in a sense of responsibility – that's fine. We can be an effective leader, providing we don't fake a level of joy that we don't feel.

Be aware, too, if we find that our mix is dramatically skewed toward one or another of these four elements with the others registering zero. If we're motivated entirely by duty, then we may over time, stick with a particular job for far longer than we should, or stay with a company solely out of a sense of obligation. If we're motivated entirely by joy, more power to you, but it wouldn't hurt to check in with the big picture to ensure that our work is in balance with our life and that our bills are getting paid!

The point is this: While any combination of the four elements is okay; extremes can be dangerous, but if we know why we're doing what we're doing, then we stand a fair chance of being able to carry that honesty through all aspects of our work.

When we know ourselves well – when we understand what drives us to work – when we can acknowledge our strengths and weaknesses – when we can let others know what to expect and what not to expect, from us in different situations – when we seek help from others to handle situations in which our own natural tendencies don't serve us well – then we will feel like an effective manager. And others will feel that way about us as well.

In other words, self-knowledge and the willingness to work within our boundaries will manifest itself into the kinds of characteristics and competencies that others will consider when they're deciding whether or not to put their trust in us. What are those characteristics and competencies? They are: *credibility, reliability, the ability to get personal and a lack of self orientation.*

The idea is to either – be strong in all four areas or be so outstanding in one that we make up for any relative shortcomings in the others.

Credibility

The short definition is 'expertise'. Do we know enough about whatever it is we're working on or talking about to warrant others' confidence in us? The right trust-building answer *doesn't* have to be "Yes, I'm an expert," but the right answer *can* be "Yes, I am an expert," if we do in fact have the knowledge. But it can also be, "No, I don't know a lot about this topic, but I know exactly where to find the information we need."

What makes someone credible inside an organization? Chances are, it's a combination of experience, the way in which someone has handled themselves in the past or their track record of tasks accomplished and how well known all of those things are throughout the organization. This last point is key. Credibility with clients is usually built with one other person (the client). But inside an organization, people cast far larger shadows because they have relationships with many people and also because those people have relationships with one another. We may be credible, but the internal 'spin' on our credibility is of equal – and sometimes greater importance.

Think of the department head, as they step to the podium at a company gathering and seem to trigger a wave of restlessness throughout the audience. The people who don't know this person personally see that, and their impressions begin to form.

What can we do to bolster our credibility? First, make it a point to give credit where credit is due. Be upfront about what we know and don't know. Be upfront about where you're going to go for the expertise you don't have. Second, develop a network of people we can go to for the expertise we don't have. We need to know how to get our hands on the right tools. A note of caution – we must ensure our network is legitimate. Dropping names will not serve us well – remember don't fake it!

Reliability

Reliability is all about being consistent and dependable. In that way, it sets itself apart from the other variables because reliability is largely about action. But it has an emotional aspect as well. Reliability, as part of the trust equation, also has to do with whether a person is able to deliver their consistency and dependability in a way that makes the receiver comfortable.

Some obvious reliability killers are constantly changing our schedule thereby affecting others or showing up late, being ill prepared or missing meetings altogether, or overpromising what we're able to deliver. And perhaps the biggest problem for many leaders is changing focus, apparently on a whim.

Less obvious, but equally poisonous, is constantly using a fixed or standard set of phrases. Or having only one set of solutions, regardless of what the problem might be.

Getting Personal

We're not suggesting that we need to share the private details of our life – or ask the same from others – in order to be an effective leader. Getting personal doesn't have to mean private. We're talking about being intensely personal about the work at hand. That is, taking to heart any serious personnel issues such as, compensation, promotion and hiring and firing people. Think of the number of lives that are affected each day by business issues ranging from one person's small promotion to a major change in organization or ownership. Think of how what we do affects other people, inside the office and in their lives outside of work. Business is personal and effective leaders never forget it.

What getting personal really means is the understanding of personal motivations, situations and sensitivities. It means getting close, emotionally, to the issues we and our employees face as we work together.

Our ability to get personal within our work, not only gives others a clearer picture of where we stand, but it can also help us spot others in our organization who might be trying to *fake it* to get by and we can help them get back on track.

Lack of Self-Orientation

Our level of self-orientation has a lot to do with what's motivating us. If our work doesn't interest us – if our motivation is coming mostly from the duty or achievement areas – chances are that we're going to focus more on ourselves when we're interacting with other people. It's a natural fall-back. But if that's the case, it's time to take a hard look about whether or not we belong in our current job.

Leadership Skills and Behaviors

The following leadership skills have been shown to be characteristic of many successful leaders.

The Successful Leader

Gives clear work instructions – communicates well in general and keeps other informed.

Praises others when they deserve it – understands the importance of recognition and looks for opportunities to build the esteem of others.

Is willing to take time to listen to others – is sensitive to the powerful effect of good listening, both for building a cooperative relationship and avoiding tension and grievances.

Is calm and cool most of the time – maintains emotional control in almost any situation and can be counted on to behave maturely and appropriately.

Has confidence and self assurance – is never arrogant or inappropriately boastful.

Has appropriate technical knowledge of the work being managed – uses this knowledge to coach, teach and evaluate rather than getting involved in the 'doing' of the work.

Understands the group's problems – demonstrates this by careful and attentive listening and by honestly trying to put themselves in another person's situation.

Gains the group's respect – this is accomplished through honesty with the group and by avoiding to try to appear more knowledgeable than is true or having the courage to say, "I made a mistake."

Is fair to everyone – this is demonstrated through the pattern of work assignments with consistent enforcement of rules, policies and procedures and avoidance of favoritism.

Demands good work from everyone – maintains consistent standards of performance and enforces work discipline.

Gains people's trust – this is demonstrated by the leader's willingness to represent the group to 'higher management' regardless of their agreement or disagreement with them.

Goes to bat for the group – will work for the best and fair interests of the work group and will not avoid approaching 'higher management' when necessary. They have loyalties to both higher management *and* the work group.

Is approachable – maintains a relationship of friendliness but is not necessarily a friend.

Is easy to talk to – demonstrates a desire to understand without tuning out feedback through criticizing, judging or belittling.

Who Should Not be a Leader

The following characteristics have shown to be present in very ineffective leaders.

One who lacks character and integrity.

One whose vision focuses on peoples' weaknesses rather than their strengths – one who is keenly aware of what each person *cannot* do rather than what they *can* do well.

One who does not believe that most people are capable of significant accomplishments or have the ability to succeed.

One who is more interested in the question, "Who is right?", rather than "What is right?"

One who is threatened by strong subordinates.

One who does not set high standards for their own work.

To be an effective leader, we need to ensure that we follow most or all of the characteristics of effective leadership listed above and we must avoid at all costs, the characteristics of ineffective leadership.

In the next section of this book, we will begin to identify the practical strategies to add to our existing value-driven leadership practices.

"We can't do really big things everyday. If we're really serious about walking the talk, we have to focus on the small stuff."

__Practical Strategies__

Develop and Maintain Technical Knowledge

"Knowledge is the only instrument of production that is not subject to diminishing returns."

❖ Dedicate a minimum of two hours per week to enhancing your technical knowledge. Consider activities such as reading, observing, listening and doing. The key here is dedicated time and focus.

❖ Divide and conquer. Work as a team to stay abreast of technological advancements. For example:
1. Divide the reading of trade and professional journals among your work group and request they add comments or highlight key information prior to linking the publication to others.

2. Ask others to share key learning from all workshops, seminars and conferences they attend.

❖ Volunteer for projects that will likely increase your knowledge, skills, marketability and value to the organization.

❖ Actively participate in one or more professional associations. Most groups offer on-line newsletters or journals, monthly meetings and opportunities to network with others in you profession. These groups provide a great opportunity to keep up with new developments, usually for a reasonable membership fee.

Adopt an Attitude for Action and Results

"Don't wait for someone else to make all the calls."

❖ Focus on results oriented processes and outcomes that add value to the organization, rather than on 'staying busy' activities and events that merely consume time.

❖ Create a list of desired results when planning tasks and projects. By evaluating potential activities against this list you will maintain focus and increase your chances of achieving the results you want.

❖ Go on a Work Safari once a week: Hunt for an important task that needs to be done...and do it. Then place it in an imaginary trophy case. You will soon develop a reputation as a great hunter.

❖ Tackle important tasks first, even though they may be ones you would least like to do. Save the fun work as a reward for handling the tougher issues.

Expect Top Performance

"Not failure, but low aim, is the problem."

❖ Be aware of the self-fulfilling prophecy:
   When you expect something to happen (positive or negative),
   you unconsciously act in a manner which makes it more likely
   to occur.

❖ Involve your team in setting standards that are
   achievable but also require them to stretch their
   knowledge and skills. Avoid settling for mediocre sub-par
   work. Remember that regardless of what you say, it is the
   performance you are willing to accept that becomes your
   true standard.

❖ Think of each member of your work group as a high
   jumper. Celebrate the reaching of new heights, then "raise
   the bar" together. But don't forget, as you are raising the
   bar, so is your competition.

❖ Make sure you walk the talk and earn the right to hold
   others to high standards by meeting them yourself.

Commit to Quality and Improvement

"There is always room for improvement – it's the biggest room in the house."

❖ Adopt the 10% Rule – set a personal goal to improve everything you are involved in, by 10 percent. Small improvements add up quickly.

❖ Focus on people as well as processes. Keep in mind that quality is ultimately a matter of individual performance. It happens one day at a time, one person at a time.

❖ Recognize and reward those who make improvements to products, processes and services. Remember: What gets celebrated gets repeated.

❖ Sponsor a local Art Show. Ask each person in your group to contribute a visual representation of what quality and continuous improvement means/looks like to them. Then display the "works of art" in a common area. This creative exercise is a fun way to involve everyone in reinforcing the quality message.

Be Customer Driven

"It's not the employer who pays the wages. Employers only handle the money. It's the customer who pays the wages."

❖ Adopt the following mind set:
1). Everyone you interact with is either an internal customer or an external customer.

2). If your customers ever stop needing you, so will your organization.

❖ Tell horror stories. Share personal examples of receiving poor service along with the impact it had on both customer and the service provider. Discuss what could have turned them into success stories.

❖ Deliver what the customer actually wants, rather than what you think they should have. If you are not sure what they want, ask!

❖ Build business partnerships with your customers by under-promising, over-delivering and following-up to ensure they are satisfied. Solicit their input on how your products and services can be improved.

Commit to Self-Development

"You should not think much of a man who is not wiser today than he was yesterday."

❖ Become a Continuous Learning Machine. Set a personal goal to learn something new about your job, your organization or your professional discipline every week.

❖ Encourage others to pursue self-development activities. Make time and resources available for them to enhance their job skills.

❖ Learn by teaching. Volunteer as an instructor for organizational training programs. You will not only develop in-depth knowledge about subjects you prepare to teach, you will also be able to help others develop and grow.

❖ Look beyond your profession. Consider pursuing developmental activities that have nothing to do with your job, but can help you grow as a person. You will probably be surprised to find that unrelated learning can positively impact your job performance.

Make Timely and Value-Driven Decisions

"The true purpose of our value statements is to guide both our behaviors and our decisions."

❖ Avoid the decision making extremes:

Knee Jerk Decisions – acting too quickly without considering alternatives or all of the facts.

Paralysis Analysis – stalling a decision with too much analysis and research.

❖ Involve those who must implement decisions in the decision making process. Consider the ideas and opinions of those who do the work, because they frequently know best and have a lot to contribute. In addition, they will be more likely to support decisions that they helped make.

❖ Ensure your decisions are in sync with organizational values before you implement them. If there is a conflict, pursue alternatives that are a better match to the stated values.

❖ When announcing a decision, always explain the reason for it as well as the process used to arrive at it.

"Words to live by are just words, unless you live by them. Set a good example for others."

Solve Problems Effectively

"Additional problems are the offspring of poor solutions."

❖ Adopt the 'Solution-Plus-One Rule' – develop and consider at least two solutions for every issue or problem.

❖ Conduct a pro vs. con analysis on all proposed solutions. Consider all relevant facts, issues and perceptions. Eliminate those with significantly more downsides.

❖ Avoid negative returns by making sure the ultimate cost of the solution (money, time, effect on others, etc.) is less than the cost of the problem.

❖ Search for winning solutions whenever possible. Adopt those solutions through which the most people are positively affected and the fewest negatively affected.

Be Flexible

"In life, change is inevitable. In business, change is vital."

❖ Encourage others to break tradition when appropriate, in order to find better ways of doing things. Remember – if you continue doing what you have always done, you will continue to get the same results.

❖ Understand and appreciate that others may not do things exactly as you would do them. Be open-minded, you might discover their way is even better.

❖ Remove 'Stop Signs to Progress' by avoiding statements such as "We've tried that before…" or "That's not the way we do things here…"

❖ Do not cast all decisions in cement. Be willing to modify them as changing circumstances or data dictate.

Support Risk Taking

"Behold the turtle. It makes progress only when it sticks its neck out."

❖ Develop a common, shared definition for intelligent risk taking to be used as a guideline for future activities.

❖ Identify specific behaviors that encourage risk taking and those that discourage it. Make a commitment to adopt encouraging behaviors and ask others to do the same.

❖ Turn failures into developmental experiences by asking, "What's positive about this? What have we learned that will help us do better in the future?"
Bottom line: Make it okay to fail.

❖ Recognize and celebrate intelligent risk taking no matter the outcome. Make it something to brag about. Consider establishing an Intelligent Risk Taker of the Month Award.

Resolve Disputes Fairly

"The mark of a well managed organization is not the absence of problems, but whether or not problems are effectively resolved."

❖ Remember that 'stuff' happens! Disputes are a natural outcome of individuals working together. So expect problems...and accept the challenge of resolving them as an opportunity to eliminate obstacles to organizational effectiveness.

❖ Make sure your 'open door' is really open. Encourage members of your group to bring to bring their major complaints to you, but don't become defensive when they do.

❖ Thoroughly investigate all complaints and make a sincere effort to resolve them as quickly as possible. Handle them as your top priority on any given day as that's exactly what they are to the people involved in them.

❖ Focus on *what's* right rather than *who's* right. Do not let unrelated issues bias your decisions.

Positively Manage Crisis Situations

"A diamond is a chunk of coal that was created under pressure."

❖ Approach crises as a team. Allow everyone to 'own a piece' of the problem. Do not be an over protective parent by trying to shield them. Capitalize on individual strengths and give everyone the opportunity to contribute to the solution.

❖ Critically assess your behavior and request feedback from others on how you handle crisis situations. Take responsibility for setting the example. Realize that others will assume its okay to respond to a crisis the same way you do.

❖ Over-communicate to keep others informed and grind down the rumor mill.

❖ Conclude each crisis with a post mortem celebration. Review what happened, identify key learning that can be applied in the future and celebrate the accomplishment of getting through it together.

"People hear what we say, but they see what we do. And seeing is believing."

Provide Recognition

"There are two things that people want more than sex and money – recognition and praise."

❖ Be a 'Star Catcher'. Regularly catch people doing things right and recognize them for it. Make recognition self-perpetuating by recognizing those who recognize others. Remember – what gets recognized gets reinforced and what gets reinforced gets repeated.

❖ Develop a list of at least 10 ways to recognize others for their performance and contributions. Some ideas to get you started: a Thank You Card with a hand written message, small gift, special assignment, etc...

❖ Customize the recognition you provide. Ask each member of your team how you can best demonstrate your appreciation for them. Then provide 'different strokes for different folks'.

❖ Let everyone 'hold the trophy'. Be sure each contributing member shares in the recognition for the group's achievements.

Conduct one-on-one meetings regularly

Offer feedback and assistance

Avoid overlooking the "middle stars"

Create an "everyone's a coach" environment

Help others succeed

Coach Others

"Coaching isn't an addition to a leader's job – it's the core part of it."

❖ Pay attention to 'middle stars'. Avoid the trap of focusing only on the 'super stars' – those with exceptional performance and the 'fallen stars' – those with significant performance problems. Most people shine somewhere in the middle.

❖ Schedule a short meeting with each of your direct Reports once every two or three weeks. Discuss their work in progress, provide feedback on how their doing and ask how you and others can contribute to their success.

❖ Go back to school! Read articles and books, attend webinars and workshops that deal specifically with coaching techniques. Then apply what you learn.

❖ Build a strong coaching environment. Begin by identifying the characteristics and behaviors exhibited by good coaches. Then ask everyone for their commitment to practice those behaviors. Consider providing coaching skills training to help each person assume their new coaching role.

       C – Conduct one-on-one meetings regularly

       O – Offer feedback and assistance

       A – Avoid overlooking the 'middle stars'

       C – Create a strong coaching environment

       H – Help others succeed

Minimize Obstacles

"All too frequently, employees do good work in spite of the organization and its leadership, rather than because of them."

❖ Ask each member of your group to identify the three most significant obstacles to their performance. Create a master list and develop a strategy to eliminate them and most importantly reward people for identifying obstacles. They have made a significant contribution by identifying ways you can add value and assist the organization.

❖ If you don't control an obstacle your group is facing, talk to people that do. Point out the impact and cost of the problem and discuss possible solutions. Even if you can't eliminate an obstacle, you may be able to minimize its effect by showing people how to get it around it easier and less painfully.

❖ Ask others what you may or may not be doing that creates obstacles for them. If they tell you, thank them for their honesty, don't get defensive but do something to eliminate the obstacles you are creating.

❖ Benchmark the best. Study industries, organizations and individuals who beat the competition by overcoming challenges and obstacles. Equally as important – review case studies of those who did not...and lost.

Provide Feedback

"Feedback is the breakfast of champions."

❖ Be certain that each person who reports to you fully understands your performance expectations. Feedback is most effective when people know the standards against which their performance is being measured.

❖ Develop the habit of giving each member of your team some type of feedback every week. If you might forget, put an ongoing reminder in your e-calendar.

❖ Make sure the feedback you provide passes the TIPS Test:

Timely: given as soon as possible after the performance takes place.

Individualized: tailored to the feedback receiver.

Productive: focuses on the performance rather than the performer.

Specific: pinpoints observable action and behaviors.

❖ While providing feedback, be also aware of your non-verbal feedback. Keep in mind that body language often communicates stronger messages than words.

Apply Rules Fairly and Consistently

"If employees understand the reasons behind the rules and regulations, the chances are excellent that they will respect them."

❖ Make certain everyone understands the importance of, and the reasons for, the specific details of rules and policies.

❖ As a group, define the terms *fairness* and *consistency* as they relate to policy and rule application. Use those definitions as guidelines for yourself and others.

❖ Do not ignore 'bad' rules and policies. Instead, try to get them changed. Be sure you are fully prepared when proposing a change. Explain why the rule is problematic, describe how it negatively impacts business and offer at least two alternatives for consideration.

❖ Create a list of 'Rules of the Road' – treating others with respect, practicing open and honest communication, etc... and treat these equally as important as all other rules.

Address Deficiencies

"No one enjoys addressing others' deficiencies. But failure to do so sends the message that people are on track when they really are not. This could be the greatest disservice a leader can do to someone else."

❖ Pay attention when someone has a performance problem. Unaddressed deficiencies can have a negative effect on every member of your team. By dealing with performance issues as early as possible, you can prevent them from growing more serious and embarrassing for both you and the individual.

❖ Investigate each deficiency to uncover its root cause. If the problem stems from a lack of skills, arrange for skill-building activities – formal   training, on the job training, etc... If there is an obstacle to performance, attempt to eliminate it. If you believe the person can perform properly, but just isn't doing so, review the standard with them and hold them accountable for meeting it.

❖ Follow-up for follow through! Follow-up the initial performance discussion with one or two short meetings to assess the individual's progress and encourage them to follow through with the correction.

❖ Treat people as adults – never assume total responsibility for correcting someone else's deficiencies. If you alone take the responsibility, they have now become non-responsible.

"Vision without action is meaningless."

Use Discipline Appropriately

"Little value comes out of the belief that people will respond progressively better by treating them progressively worse."

❖ Try a positive approach to discipline. Focus on correction and individual responsibility rather than blame and punishment. Avoid perspectives such as *write you up* and *punishment that fits the crime.*

❖ When holding disciplinary discussions, concentrate on the particular problem and its impact on the business. Deal with specific facts and behaviors rather than personalities or attitudes. This will help decrease defensiveness and produce value-added outcomes.

❖ Never document a disciplinary problem without talking to the person about the issue. A good rule of thumb – if it's important enough to document, it's definitely important enough to talk about.

❖ Apply discipline effectively by ensuring that:

1). Your process and decisions are fair and consistent.

2). Your overall objective is to build commitment rather than mandate compliance.

Perform With Integrity

"If leaders are careless about basic things like telling the truth, respecting moral codes, or proper professional conduct – who can believe them on other issues."

❖ Everyone must play by the same rules. Rank has its privileges and may apply in some circumstances, but never when it comes to integrity issues.

❖ Nobody's perfect – we all make mistakes and errors in judgment. Admit to them and apologize for any negative impacts they may have caused. How you recover from mistakes is a true indication of your integrity.

❖ Be a person of your word. Write down all promises and agreements you make and honor them. Remember – one broken promise overshadows five promises kept.

❖ Let your conscience be your guide. Do the right thing no matter how inconvenient, unpopular or painful it may seem. That is integrity.

Support Organizational Values

"It's critical that managers ensure their departments are about what we say about our company."

❖ Provide everyone with a copy of your organization's value statements. Adopt the mind set that value statements are part of your work rules and treat them accordingly.

❖ Develop a list of ways to recognize and reward employees for behavior that corresponds with organizational values. Continue until you have 10 ways - then start doing them.

❖ When planning projects and activities, write down what you intend to accomplish then add the phrase..."in a way that supports and furthers our organizational values." Evaluate your final plans against this, add-on criteria.

Accept and Meet Responsibilities

"The price of greatness is responsibility."

❖ Ensure everyone's responsibilities, including yours, are clearly defined and commonly understood. Whether it's a specific project or general job duty, do not assume people know who is responsible for what...discuss it.

❖ Be selfish. Never share the blame for your mistakes.

❖ Volunteer to take on additional responsibilities – especially when no one else wants it. It may temporarily result in more work for you and your group, but it is also a chance to develop individuals and have a greater influence on important outcomes for your organization. Your gesture just might inspire others to do the same.

❖ Check the mirror first. Meet your responsibilities before holding others accountable for meeting theirs.

Handle Authority Appropriately

"Being powerful is like being a nice person. If you have to tell people you are, you aren't."

❖ Adopt the mind set that your employees do not work for you – you work for them. Refer to your group as *"the people I work for."*

❖ Avoid 'my way or the highway' thinking and behaviors. They are counterproductive and limit the possibilities of discovering new and better ways to do things. Your competitors just may be looking to pick up those hitchhikers.

❖ Complete the sentence: "I do my most effective work for leaders who..." List as many answers as possible and use this list as your guide to leading others.

❖ Remember that with authority, comes the responsibility to use it wisely and to the benefit of your entire team. Your organization can give you a leadership title, but only you can earn it.

Empower Others

"The best leader is the one who has sense enough to pick good people to do what he or she wants done and the self-restraint to keep from interfering with them while they do it."

❖ Share authority. Let each person be the owner of something meaningful – a process, a database, a piece of equipment, etc... Having ultimate authority changes the scope and perception of a responsibility that is already part of the job description.

❖ Create opportunities for non-managerial people to shine. Invite them to participate in task forces and project teams. The frequently untapped potential of this group is one of your organization's greatest weapons.

❖ Never turn your back on people after giving them authority. Instead, increase communication, feedback and interaction. Make sure they understand the parameters and expectations of that authority. Help them be successful by providing the resources and support they need.

❖ Speak 'Empower-ese'. Add statements like the following to your vocabulary:

> "Would you like to take the lead on this one?"
>
> "How can I best support you?"
>
> "It's your call."
>
> "I trust your judgment."

Together

Everyone

Achieves

More

Support Teamwork

"None of us is as smart as all of us."

❖ Accept the reality that team approaches may take longer, but usually add more value and produce better results in the long run.

❖ Make teamwork a stated performance expectation. Involve others in compiling a list of factors and characteristics critical to effective team work. Hold people accountable for cooperative behaviors and for contributing to each others success.

❖ Provide training to help individuals work more effectively in teams. Do not assume that people can or will work as a team only because you have labeled them as one.

❖ Recruit and select people who have teamwork behaviors. It's difficult enough to change attitudes and behaviors of existing employees by adding new human obstacles.

   T – Together
   E – Everyone
   A – Achieves
   M – More

Enhance the Work Environment

"The quality of employees will be directly proportional to the quality of life you maintain for them."

❖ Hold everyone accountable for doing their jobs so that no one has to pick up the slack for the others.

❖ Ask fellow workers to submit three ideas each for enhancing the quality of work life in your area. Create a master list of ideas and start implementing the easiest ones as quickly as possible.

❖ Make 'quality of life' a regular agenda item at group meetings. Solicit feedback on how the group is doing and where you can make improvements.

❖ Recruit someone to be your group's 'Ambassador of Fun'. Make appropriate resources available for them to help bring enjoyment to the workplace. Consider rotating the responsibility every three months.

See the Big Picture

"You have got to think about 'big things' while you are doing small things so that all the small things go in the right direction."

❖ Everything that you and your team does either adds value and supports your organization's mission, or it doesn't. Do not allow any opportunity for people to question the value of your contributions.

❖ Identify and consider all sides of an issue prior to making a decision or planning work activities. Ask yourself – "How will this action effect other departments, individuals, customers and the organization as a whole?"

❖ Involve others in developing a mission statement for your business unit. Make sure it's in-line with your organization's overall mission and describes your unit's specific contribution and supporting activities.

❖ Take a field trip. Let your team see the big picture for themselves by visiting other departments within your company and also the end users of your products and services.

Be Enthusiastic

"If you are working for a company that is not enthusiastic, energetic, creative, clever, curious and just plain fun, you have serious troubles."

❖ Get excited about positive things. If you are normally calm and reserved, pick something you are 'fired-up' about and act yourself into excitement. Initiate enthusiasm and the feeling will follow.

❖ Think of the most enthusiastic person you know. Ask them to share their secrets to maintaining an enthusiastic outlook. Then practice those secrets and pass them along to others.

❖ Spread the sparkle. Get enthused about others who are enthusiastic – it is contagious and can snowball quickly. Recognize and reward those who contribute to a culture of contagious enthusism.

"Values are the gold that's in each of us. They're the real fortune of any organization."

Display Resilience

"It's not whether you get knocked down it's whether you get up."

When facing disappointment or frustration:

❖ Take a deep breath, slowly count to ten and think about how you want to affect others – your responsibility is to lead people out of disappointment rather than into it.

❖ Take a hike – go on a ten minute walk to calm down, reflect and develop a bounce back strategy.

❖ Maintain the proper perspective – it is not the end of the world so do not act like it is. Find one or two positives then move on to other tasks.

Show Concern for Others

"When people work in a place that cares about them, they contribute a lot more than duty."

❖ Remember special occasions. Send cards with personalized messages to your fellow workers on special days such as birthdays and anniversaries with the organization.

❖ Regularly spend one-on-one time with each member of your team. Open these informal get-togethers with a general questions like – "How are things going with you"? Then really listen to what they have to say. Listening is an important way to demonstrate that you care.

❖ Whenever possible, help people balance work needs and personal needs. A little consideration and flexibility on your part can go a long way in showing you care for others beyond what they can produce on the job.

❖ Periodically, 'tag along' with members of your team and observe first hand the issues and problems they face. You will be able to see things from their perspective and develop the empathy important to caring for others.

Solicit and Apply Feedback from Others

"Truly great leaders spend as much time collecting and acting on feedback as they do providing it."

❖ Do not wait for your annual performance appraisal to collect feedback on your performance. Ask your boss to meet with you at least once per quarter to discuss how you are doing.

❖ Ask others in your circle of influence to become partners in your efforts for continuous improvement. Regularly solicit feedback on how you are perceived. Then seek out a 'coaching buddy' to help you sort through this information and develop action plans to increase your effectiveness.

❖ Keep a feedback log. Dedicate a page in your daily calendar to record feedback you receive from others and the specific things you will do to act upon the feedback. Review the log at the beginning of each week.

❖ Circulate selected first draft work of your action plan to the appropriate individuals with a request for upgrade suggestions. Try to include as many ideas as possible into your final product. Do not forget to show your appreciation for their time and contributions. You will get a better product and grow your relationships with others.

Manage Time

"Time is the scarcest resource we have and unless it is managed, nothing else can be managed."

❖ Target the time wasters. Work together with your group to identify all inefficient uses of time existing within your area. Select the three most significant items and develop a joint strategy for eliminating or minimizing them.

❖ Delegate important tasks you do not have time to do. Just make sure you are not creating unnecessary work for others. Everyone is responsible for helping everyone else manage their time effectively.

❖ Tackle your in-box every other day instead of every day. Focus on completing the really important items rather than trying to stay caught up each day. Ask others to tag their 'hot' emails with a special subject line if it cannot wait.

❖ Go on vacation – in the office. Isolate yourself in order to work on critical projects and ask others to handle issues as if you really were gone. Clear it with your boss and ask for their cooperation in honoring your 'time off.'

"Good things happen when you make sure that good things happen."

Manage Meetings

"The form of the meeting is simply a reflection of the culture."

❖ Does it make sense to have a meeting? Do not have a meeting if there is a more cost effective way to achieve your objective. Ask others to help you develop a list of ways to accomplish tasks with minimal need for group meetings. Just for fun – calculate the total cost of your last meeting including salaries and other expenses to see if you got your money's worth.

❖ Supply all participants with a written agenda three or four days prior to a meeting. Make sure the agenda includes the meeting objective, issues to be discussed, start/end times, location, who will be attending, how participants should prepare and what they should bring.

❖ Manage the meeting. Establish ground rules upfront, including a list of 'do' and 'don't' meeting behaviors. Then keep the group on track, follow the ground rules and adhere to the time frame. If you manage the process, the results will take care of themselves.

❖ End all meetings with a short review of results. Discuss what was accomplished and what needs to be followed-up on after the meeting.

Communicate Effectively

"How well we communicate is determined not by how well we say things, but how well we are understood."

❖ Think before you speak and plan before you write. Understand your message before expecting others to. Target your communication to the intended audience by using terminology they are likely to understand. Consider pre-testing important communications on individuals who will give you candid feedback.

❖ Be concise and specific. Avoid ambiguous words and phrases that may mean different things to different people – words like, "usually", "sometimes", "a lot", "rarely", etc.

❖ Try communicating creatively with stories, examples, pictures, videos, etc...to help convey your message and increase retention.

❖ Never assume others understand what you say or write – check to be sure. Ask them to describe their understanding of your message. This will allow you to clarify and correct any misunderstandings.

Keep Others Informed

"If you do not give people information, they will make up something to fill the void."

❖ Establish a 'No Surprise Rule' for yourself and others. Make withholding bad news the absolute worse violation of all.

❖ Do not be an 'information hoarding' power broker. Ask each member of your group to identify the type and amount of information that would help them be more successful – then make sure they get it.

❖ Regularly update your boss and colleagues on your activities and progress. If anyone has a problem with where you are headed, you will find out before going too far down the wrong path.

❖ Choose a high traffic area and designate it as 'Information Central'. Provide a suitably sized bulletin board for displaying activities in progress, results, project status, production data, new products and other general information.

Listen to Others

"It is impossible to think that we listen only with our ears. It is much more important to listen with the mind, the eyes, the body and the heart. Unless you truly want to understand the other person, you will never be able to listen."

❖ Give the speaker your conscious attention. Maintain eye contact and listen for feelings as well as words. This will help you absorb the full extent of their communication and make them feel important at the same time.

❖ If you are not sure what you have heard – paraphrase – repeat back in your own words what the person said. Paraphrasing typically begins with... "What I hear you saying is..." and ends with..."Is that correct?"

❖ Never interrupt someone when they are speaking. Never plan what you will say while they are speaking. Never assume you are listening because you can hear.

Taking Care of You

"It is very difficult to achieve great success if one does not have complete balance in their lives."

Intellectual

Financial   Physical

YOU

Spiritual   Family

Social

Give the above categories equal weighting in your life to help you achieve complete balance. You will be surprised by the results!

Intellectual: Reading
                      Conferences/Seminars
                      Courses

Physical: Exercise
                      Diet
                      Wellness

Financial: Professional/Business
                      Personal/Budget
                      Retirement

Family: Family Time
                      Special Activities
                      Holidays

Social: Friends
                      Unstructured Time
                      Special Activities

Spiritual: Private
                      Family
                      Congregational

Epilogue

This acclaimed management book presents the cornerstone of leadership philosophy. With a manageable page count for on-the-go readers, it is full of proven ideas and strategies for practicing value-added leadership. Everyone from corporate executives to individuals with leadership responsibilities will benefit from this easy to read, quick reference guide. The objective of this book is to keep the message simple and for you to use it again and again for reference throughout your days, months and years.

The key to effective leadership lays not in what we do, but in who we are.

www.ingramcontent.com/pod-product-compliance
Lightning Source LLC
Chambersburg PA
CBHW071635170526
45166CB00003B/1329